A SHIP PORTRAIT

MICMAC, SHIP

1853

A SHIP PORTRAIT

A NOVELLA‑IN‑VERSE

Harry Thurston

GASPEREAU PRESS

PRINTERS & PUBLISHERS

Kentville, Nova Scotia

2005

"It is like trying to paint a soul."

JOHN RUSKIN

"Of Truth of Water," *Modern Painters*

"The study of beauty is a duel in which the
artist cries out in terror before being vanquished."

CHARLES BAUDELAIRE

"Confiteor of the Artist," *Petits poèmes en prose*

"… life is shipwreck in the end."

PETER EVERETT

The Voyages of Alfred Wallis

I've been looking for you, O'Brien,
—too late, I know,
dead already a hundred years—
I've been looking so long
for one like you, not an iron man,
a tar afloat on a wooden ship,
but one who dreamed a golden age,
hands dipped in the sea's palette.
One like me, marooned ashore,
an onlooker telescoping history.
I've been looking for you, O'Brien,
finally found you, coughing up your life
in the Poor House, still waiting for your ship
to come in. That's the way it's been,
ever since you left us, O'Brien,
a long looking back. The ships are gone
but for the ones your brushes christened.

7 SEPTEMBER 1891

At first I heard only the wind whistling
through the wires, a moaning that might have been
my own pained breath labouring in my throat;
then the rains began drumming on the roof
like soldiers on parade at the Citadel;
the alarm was ringing; the brass vibrating
through my body like a tropical fever.

Top hats became black bats,
airborne alley cats crashed through windows,
power arced across Spring Garden Road,
branding the air with fireworks; trees toppled,
as if the earth had been dismasted,
roots upturned like the keels of capsized barques.
Bawdy houses quaked
on Barrack Street, bricks flew down Barrington,
awnings were ripped like unreefed sails in a cyclone—
the city foundered like the derelict ships
you painted late in life.

Anchors dragged, the schooner *Wenonah*
drifted ashore, the new yacht *Youla*
slipped her moorings, sinking boats in her wake,
the *J. L. Crossley* went down, coal and all,
lay on her side, a wreck.

Like me, like all men, at life's end.

I was born at sea, slipped my mother
into the slop of a worm-eaten ship.
My first cries mingled with turr and tickleace—
the Grand Banks, halfway between the Green Island
and the New World. I was Janus looking both ways,
one more starving mouth fleeing the English blight.
Some say this is myth, self-made to increase my fame.
Some say it was another John O'Brien
(a common enough name) who was sea-born,
or even a brother, stillborn, a dark
double to follow me all my days.
But it was I, John O'Brien, Artist,
who was first rocked in the bowels of a ship,
who came ashore, newborn, in Saint John town.

So what if you were not born at sea?
Art is myth making, memory becoming,
regardless of history.
The artist's is a life lived backwards.

My father Daniel named me well—
John Daniel O'Connell O'Brien.
I was the namesake of the Liberator,
Daniel O'Connell. Like him
I came from a fine stock of sea people,
my father from Cork, his from Kerry,
ship wreckers, kin to the Jacobites,
    enemies of the Saxons—
there was no end to our troubles.

No man could enter a learned profession,
No man could hold any public office,
No man could establish an industry
    with more than two apprentices,
No man could acquire any property.
Any Orangeman could hijack your horse
    for five quid.

Then came the Liberator, eloquent:
"Your native land shall be a country of strangers,"
    he said.
"You shall be aliens in the soil that gave you birth,"
    he said
"Only foreigners may attain rank, station, honours,"
    he said.

And then O'Connell changed all that,
taking his seat in Westminster,
grit under the heel of Dublin Castle.

My dear father named me well, but the Troubles
followed us here like stowaway black rats.

"The altar of freedom must not be cemented
with blood, supported by carcasses,"
          he said.

Legislate as you will; for me
Art was the only Liberator.

As boys we were urchins of Water Street.
It smelt of salt cod, black rum, tar and tea.
Irishtown they called it, where my countrymen
rubbed shoulders with Negroes, clapped each other's back.
You could buy a needle or an anchor.
Without a penny, we came to learn the sails.

There seemed no end to the cut of sails
for ship, barque, brigantine, schooner, anchored
at the docks. They carried molasses and tea
from Caribe and China. On Water Street
lorries hauled it all away, while men
carted their sea-chests on their backs
       like barnacles.

Head over heel, we trundled down the steep back
of Halifax town where the ships lay at anchor,
their sails furled, linen white or brown as tea.
Up and down the shrouds and masts men
scurried, black as ants, setting the sails
spread like a bank of cloud along Water Street.

Dodging horse and cart we crossed Water Street
to the wharves. Masts and spars crossed, tees
towering above us, rocking back
and forth as the great ships lay at anchor.
Mizzen, top gallant, royal, jib, all sails
we dreamt of working when we were men.

To us, sailors were the only true men.
We scorned all others behind their backs.
Not for us to trudge up whale-back streets,
to sit in parlours, shore-bound, sipping tea.
We wanted to feel the wind in our sails,
slip into faraway ports to drop anchor.

It was to the sea we looked to anchor
our dreams—sea-bound, we would never look back.
Water would divide us from lesser men
when we climbed aloft to unfurl the sails.
Poor lads would hail us from Water Street,
the words grow fainter: *Oil Clothes, Dry Goods, Tea ...*

stencilled on the chandleries. The teeming
ocean would beckon, the trades fill our sails—
not knowing if one day they would blow us back.

We still have our Water Streets
with their harping gulls, their raw smells,
but the ships are long gone.
Only the hulls of derelict draggers
litter the shore.
Wharves teeter on rotten piles
where the tall ships once berthed.
We need you, O'Brien, to bring them back,
ballasted with the exotic—

ivory backscratcher,
                    Shanghai,
peacock quill cigar case,
                    Java,
four whales teeth,
                    Indian Ocean,
wild boar tusks,
                    New Zealand,
maté cup and bombilla,
                    Buenos Aires,
opium pipe,
                    China,
ant egg necklace,
                    Cape Town,
pearl fish hook,
                    Solomon Islands,
war club,
                    Australia—

preserved under glass
like your portraits, O'Brien,
testament to our great wanderings.

Once we were cosmopolitan,
once we set our hopes like our sails,
seaward, to all points of the compass.

Once we were at home in Bombay
or Rangoon,
familiar in Melbourne
or Hong Kong,
masters wherever
our keels
cut water.

My father was an Artist in Hair,
procured the finest locks from New York.
The ladies piled them high, fake cumuli
propped on their porcelain brows.
High society donned the pawned tresses
of the poor, already bought and paid for—
even the hairs of their lousy heads.
I would wig the sky with clouds instead,
cirri, the portent of a storm worrying
   the clear blue.
Sails, you might say, were the gowns
swathing my wooden ladies of the waves.
Next to the mute, coiffed mannequins
I propped my first portraits, as did Turner,
his father like my own, a Barber.
The Dutchman, van de Velde the Younger,
hurt us both to paint—his storms at sea
wigged with white caps pulled us under.

   Boys of good character, O'Brien,
   at first we hardly knew
   what was happening
   as we felt the first tug,
   the undertow calling us
   to deeper water.

YACHT RACE, 1850

The officers got up a regatta.
Already my sketch of the flagship
and squadron southbound for Bermuda
had been celebrated in the *Nova Scotian*—
I was not yet nineteen. The clouds cleared
while the wind, N.N.W. off the land, filled
the sails but hardly rippled the harbour.
Half the town, decked out in holiday colours,
gathered at the dock. The rum and bets went down.
The *Pyramus*—Nelson's proud booty—flew
a pyramid of flags, gunnel to topmast.

Sloops, schooners, cutters and yawls tacked
about the old lady like sea⁄dancers
coupled in feverish reel or quadrille.
I kept watch to freeze this motion:
    in the fifth race
I saw what I was looking for—*Mystery*,
Eclipse, *Wanderer*, close⁄hauled on the port tack.
Looking back, these three might have been my fates.

That day I attended to the sea, set of sail,
sky and its gathering fleet of torn clouds.
What is a ship without the sky's weather?
(Even Ruskin knew that, Turner too.)
The canvas is a mirror for cloud-light.
"The rain cloud," Ruskin said, "carries its own wind.
It reveals all that is beautiful,
conceals all that is hurtful, makes the paltry
look vast, the ponderous, light and airy."

Skipper balanced on her bow, *Mystery*
tacked into the sky's dark embrace,
a foreboding my eye could not ignore.
                                Mystery heeled over,
the ivory spray scrimshawed her black hull.
Her pursuers fell off the right margin
    of my canvas.
Everything rushed away, soundless,
while the picture composed itself

—"a very clever specimen," they said.

Who knows what posterity will preserve—
something we pray? Perhaps it is not
all for naught.

My career was launched like a packet ship
bound for Australia or the China Sea.
My first commission was the *Celestial*
(well named, I thought, for my lyrical skies).
I painted her three times: first
for the Counting Room, then for the Master,
and one for a House in London. My art
clipped across the seas—"under all sail,
studding sails from main royal down."
My spirits were high, riding her name.
Good enough for the *London Illustrated News*,
the papers said, if only the harbour
scenery were glossed in more detail,
the redoubtable fort in bold relief,
if only I had a master to mould me.
Damn them. I paint their country's pride—
                                                          a ship,
that great machine of water, wind and sky—
and the merchants crow for streets, for lowly buildings.

They are lost, all three,
along with *Eclipse*, *Milo*,
Middleton and *Halifax*.
Wrecked by time,
without a trace,
surely as the ships themselves.
Eaten by moths or worms,
consumed by fire or water,
it's all the same:
the thing itself
and its image.

"THE FINE ARTS—YOUNG O'BRIEN has painted a fine
picture of the Brig, *Kaloolah*, for the enterprising owners, Salter
and Twining. The vessel is shown running out of Halifax
Harbour under all plain sail to royal and flying jib."

Fine indeed, for a young lad not yet twenty-one
to knock off two portraits in a month;
but times I wished to follow that *kaloolah*
over the dirge-like swell of the Pacific
to Typee.

Melville, that other poet of the sea,
died, like you, in penury,
in the same year, mad
as Bartleby—
"I prefer not to ..."

HALIFAX HARBOUR, SUNSET
1853

What was it I wanted to paint, you ask—
the sea (though it is only a harbour view),
the sky with its October colours,
the town encrusting the fort-crowned hill,
the ships loitering on the waves
as the sun sinks down, or the sailor
with the pike pole spearing a deadhead
as if it were a shark?—I can't remember.
The harbour was my ready canvas
      —Bedford to Sambro—
stretched daily before my eyes,
a pageant of iron, sailcloth, wood.
I plodded the planks, itinerant,
in search of a commission, patron's
largesse. Most days there was none.
Why not, then, paint the scene itself—
the nautical panorama unrolling
      like a travelling sideshow.

Foreground: the sea begins in shadow,
in depth, roiled and discontent.
The ships, frigate and merchant brig,
stand guard on either side of the canvas
      —Charybdis and Scylla—
on one side, war, on the other, commerce,
aspects of the same thing, if you ask me.
The setting sun floods city and basin,

a steamer scrawls its inky statement,
schooners tack to starboard or to port
(their sails catch the light as sharply as the wind),
the sun gilds the dome of St. George's,
as if this were Byzantium.
But it was the sky that spoke urgently—
I remember now—its last light
rising to meet the azure of descending night.
("The sky," Ruskin said, "does not remain
the same for two inches together.")
Lemon into peach, ochre into vermillion,
vermillion into ultramarine.

Look now, O'Brien,
what is familiar
in the harbour
you knew so well,
besides the corrugations
(lamp black, cobalt, purple madder),
the long susurrus of the sea,
painted with quick flicks
of the wrist, white pigment
flying from wave crests; besides
predictable gulls and cormorants,
port mascots riding the chop,
the terraced hump of George's
(abandoned but still beaconed) stepping

tentatively into the deep;
and beyond, where the sky's greyness
blends with water,
the lighthouse on Devil's Island
barely keeping its head up,
like a drowning man?
These everyday vistas
as common for you
as for us.

But look here, O'Brien:
instead of unseeable wind, the flare,
effluvia, the slick of oil in air and water.
Oil rigs jacked
above the waves
like daddy-long-legs,
drilling the sands
where so many of your ships
foundered.
Steel instead of wood: two spans
suspended in fog
in the morning,
in the afternoon
touching both shores,
the selvages of your world.
Instead of clippers

dressed in tiers of canvas,
like floating wedding cakes,
container ships, ungraceful bulks
with boxes as big as rail cars,
piled impossibly high—

not a sail in sight, O'Brien.

An alien scene but for the ultramarines,
       the soul of water,
and crazy Ruskin's vaulted skies.

"Young O'Brien, the well known Marine painter offers his
services to merchants and masters of vessels. We have often borne
testimony to the ability of this young but clever Artist, and can
confidently recommend him to the mercantile community. Not a
few of O'Brien's productions already grace the counting rooms
of this city; those which adorn the office of Geo. H. Starr, Esq,
have been very justly admired by nautical men."

I was kin to the Italian,
the Chinaman, Liverpudlian,
pierhead painters all. In every port
from Shanghai to Naples we haunted the docks,
paintbox, portfolio and testimonials
                    in tow.
We could give you a ship on even keel,
or *ex voto* for salvation from peril.
Accuracy was our stock in trade,
with a flourish of sky and sea as nod
                    to our art.
My father dressed up the port ladies' heads,
I primped captains' vanities.
Marseilles, Messina, Belfast, Antwerp,
wherever the bow pointed, there we were—
Luigi, Honoré, Joseph, Ye Shing—
like barnacles on pylons, our feathered hands
working the waves for food and drink.

There is no shame in honest craft, O'Brien,
the thing made to order.
But the purpose of art
is to make something new,
to make yourself over.

After all, the artist
paints light manifest:
the ship passing between the eye
and the sun—for an instant
illuminated, the man revealed.

MICMAC, SHIP, 1853

"The new Ship, bearing the above name, and built to run as a
regular trader between this port and the Clyde—replacing the
Clydesdale, lost last autumn on the coast of Scotland—arrived
here on Tuesday last, after a fine passage of 21 days from
Greenock. The *Mic Mac*, like all the modern ships on the
Clyde, is really a splendid vessel—measures about 375 tons,
new—is commanded by Capt. Thomas Auld, long known
and deservedly esteemed in the trade. This fine Ship is now
delivering a full cargo of Scotch goods at the Market Wharf, and
we have no doubt Consignees will receive them in as good order
as her predecessors were accustomed to land the wares of Auld
Scotia on the shores of the Scotia of the New World."

What of the trade in human cargo?
Her Irish goods were not so well
received as the wares of Auld Scotia.

And what of the people
for whom she was named,
huddled on the shores of Bedford Basin,
already blanketed with smallpox,
imprisoned like the Irish Janus
in their own land.

What darkness did she freight?
Was I condemned to memorialize
   my kin?

Irish peasants proved more profitable ballast
      than sand or bricks.
The wormy coffin ships rolled like drunkards
      across the Atlantic.
In East Indiamen that once carried tea and silk
(converted below decks, two square feet per person),
the famished curled on beds of straw.

"The Irish emigrant before he comes out
knows not what it is to lie in bed.
If you put him in a bed and give him
pork and flour, you make him sick.
But when he comes, he gets no more
than his length and breadth
upon the deck of a ship ...
And he comes out a healthy man."

Fuck Uniacke!
None of his kin ate the herbs of the field,
crammed their starved mouths
with wild mustard, dock, nettletops,
died with grasses on their lips.

Fuck Uniacke!
He never stood ankle-deep in his own shit,
in the lightless, airless lazar house of a hold,
steam rising from the human dunghill
fetid enough to knock a man over.
He never sewed his mother, son,
daughter, sister, brother, father, wife,
neighbour into a shroud of sailcloth,
dumped them overboard, food for sharks.

The Whigs starved a nation, withholding corn,
exporting grain while the "bog-trotters"
bloated and dropped, or fled to America,
flopped onto the beach like fish out of water—
and these were the lucky ones.

Here they come, through the ice,
flying their flags of sickness.
Ship fever begins as a mist in the brain,
breaks out in purple blotches,
swelling pain, pustules,
bloody flux,
a blazing thirst—

"Water, for God's sake, water!"

They die aboard ship, in the fever sheds,
or in the ghettoes of Saint John and Quebec.
Twenty-thousand in Black '47 alone.

And with them the poetry, the music,
the dancing.

"Unless the Irish go away,
  or are got rid of in some manner,
nothing good can ever be done
with that unhappy country."

Ah, yes, the final solution.

Bless you, O'Brien,
the year the Famine ends
you begin to paint.

THE SAXON, THE STAG AND THE OMAR PACHA, BARQUES, 1854–55

I was the man about town while Crimea festered,
men shipped out to Australia for gold.
Barques and brigantines to carry troops and timber
slipped from LaHave, Chester, Halifax yards—
the *Saxon*, the *Stag* and the *Omar Pacha*—
and I was there to make their builders proud.
Mine was the spyglass view from the New World,
seaward, framed by pilot ship and lighthouse.
My ships seemed to walk the star-marked waters,
"like a thing of life," the papers proclaimed.
Townsfolk and press alike clambered to praise
the bold declarations of my palette.
I walked the waterfront with a swagger,
my tall frame rocking like the mast of a ship
at anchor. My prospects were open
as the clear blue skies, touched by violet.

What happened to those water-walkers, O'Brien?
When they sailed out of your frame, out the harbour,
by Sambro, all sails set, what fate awaited them?
I'm here to tell you, though likely
you already know—gossip, the shipping news
passed along the waterfront (like bad gin)
from counting house to tavern.

The *Saxon*:
Class A2,
good enough
to ship to Peru or Chile,
around the Horn
to load guano;
built of various species
of timber, fastened with iron nails, spikes
and bolts; 299 tons, 119 feet, three-masted,
16-foot draft; sheathed with "yellow metal,"
i.e. copper, to prevent attacks
of sea worm.

A lot of good that did her!

"Monday, Nov. 11, 1861. The Barque *Saxon* of Halifax, from
Grimsby, England for Pará was totally lost on the Guriple Shoals
on April 21, the crew all saved and arrived at Pará in the boats."

Pará?

In Belém, rubber port of the great Amazon
(black balls of latex stinking in the hold),
the beached men looking for a Novascotiaman home.

The *Stag*—

Was there ever a better ship?

    cutting the Equator in record time,
    21 days out of Halifax.

    There she goes,
    off to Mauritius
    one more time

to load sugar,

    then to Coringa,
    long since silted in,
    back to Mauritius,

more sugar,

    then to Melbourne,

gold,

    back to Mauritius,

more goddamned sugar,

back to Melbourne,
across the bay
to Geelong,

sheep wool,

back to Mauritius,

yet again!

then to Clyde, Greenock,

Scotch goods,

and home to Halifax—gone
two years, five months,
less five days.

Back to Mauritius, Calcutta, Demerara …

Log of George McKenzie, Commander of the barque *Stag*
(in a fine hand)
"all sails set by the wind":

HALIFAX FOR MAURITIUS:

January 8, 1856
39° 35' S, 16° 8' E

"Strong gales with high sea.
Noon, carried away main top gallant mast.
P. M. strong gales and squally."

January 12, 1856
39° 29' S, 32° 37' E

"Sent up new Main top gallant mast."

MAURITIUS FOR CORK:

March 18, 1856
24 °43' S, 3° 33' E

"Moderate breezes and fine weather.
All sails set to best advantage.
At 10 P.M. A. Marshall departed this life."

March 19, 1856
22° 53' S, 1° 42' E

"8 a.m. committed his body to the deep.
Noon, brisk winds & fine,
passed an American ship homeward bound."

GLASGOW FOR HALIFAX:

June 29, 1856
47° 00' N, 48° 08' W

"A.M. clear, saw a large Iceberg to windward,
passed 2 bergs to leeward."

June 30, 1856
47° 04' N, 49° 56' W

"4 p.m. James Pollack fell from fore top gallant yard
to deck."

July 1, 1856
46° 25' N, 52° 01' W

"A. M. Moderate breezes & foggy.
3 a.m. James Pollack died, at 8 committed
his body to the deep.

Rain, thunder & lightning.
P. M. strong gales, with heavy seas."

MAURITIUS FOR CALCUTTA:

February 13, 1857
15° 00' S, 59° 19' E

"Hard gales with heavy rain.
Close reefed topsails.
Think we crossed in front of a cyclone."

CALCUTTA FOR DEMERARA:

June 10, 1857
36° 27' S, 22° 15' E

"Fresh breezes, 10 a.m. strong gales,
double reefs; noon, close-reefed.
4 p.m. wore ship and hove to.
6 p.m. Violent gale in topsail and lay
under bare poles, ship hove down."

June 11, 1857 "… Heavy gales with violent squalls …"
June 12, 1857 "… Strong gales with hard squalls …"
June 13, 1857 "… Strong gales with heavy squalls …"
June 14, 1857 "… Heavy gales and cloudy dark weather.
Laying to …"

June 15, 1857
37° 20' S, 26 °54' E

"Heavy gales with hail, showers.
8 p.m. wind moderate
and hauled to W. S. W.
Made sail."

HALIFAX FOR MAURITIUS:

One more time.

October 20, 1860
12° 44' N, 34° 13' W

"Moderate breezes and cloudy.
6 a.m. Andrew Bauer who has been insane
since leaving Halifax"

Who could blame him?

    "was lost overboard.
    Rounded to but the body
    sank immediately ..."

    As did the *Stag* itself,
    off Bermuda, 1863.

And what is spoken of the *Omar Pacha*?

    Condemned, 1868.

A hangashore, I was the fixed point,
the still centre, around which the great ships
revolved as they compassed the circle routes.
If they failed to return, they sailed on
    in my art.

OCEAN BRIDE, BRIGANTINE, 1854

My *Ocean Bride*, her white sails unsullied
      as a wedding gown.
I caressed the canvas like the woman
I never had. All the fine young ladies
who came and went from my father's shop,
too good, too fair, too high for one like me:
Irish. Itinerant artist. Dockside rat.

Your bride of the ocean
leaving Halifax harbour,
escorted by her maids of honour—
brig, ketch, schooner.
Still she shines, ghostly
in her gallery,
transcendent,
though her body
sank beneath the waves
long ago, 1857 to be exact.
The corkscrew worms
augered her womb,
but she will be yours,
always. This light-struck
lover.

Portrait of a Ship, 1855

Now I began to knock them off, one
every week or so. I always gave them
what they wanted—"under full sail"—
as if I were painting their own portraits.
How do men become wood, iron, hemp
        and canvas?
Or is it the wind, waves and scudding skies
we wear in our guts, on our faces?
We are all prone to becoming what we make,
captive to our own manic compass.

Show them in the harbour, landfall or departure,
either way within sight of land—lighthouse,
headland or island to port or starboard.
Show them the certainty of payoff,
the promise of good passage:
the pilot ship close by, the burden
        of navigation lifted.

The ships grow and grow,
no longer infinitesimal specks,
mere pencil crosses on the flat ocean
    of the tract chart.
They fly their house flags like badges of courage;
they are not yet lost, condemned, broken up,
    cut down or sold.
In my art they would always be whole;
for this flattery they paid me.
In my art, the winds were always propitious,
the way clear, the owners' fortune assured.
The portrait granted them what fate withholds.

Look closely at these pictures of perfection—
you may see the vanity of commerce,
but always the sky is making weather,
the sea's cruel undercurrent is pulling
the enterprise toward the patient rocks.
The violet in the clouds, each wavelet,
conjures doubt, foreshadowing disaster.

You gave them what they wanted, O'Brien,
who could blame you for that? After all
you had a living to make. You gave us
what we now need, not just the faithful record
of the ships (their cut and rig),
but an image of a better time, outward-
looking, not close-hauled against the shore,
insular.

Still we sit in judgement, spew epithets—
"primitive, hack, potboiler, provincial, naive"—
as if we did not see ourselves better
after you had portrayed us as stately ships.
In the end, when the brokers' fortunes
are spent, the heroics of iron men acted out,
what is left but your art?

THE ARAB, BRIGANTINE, AND THE MILO,
BRIG, OFF HALIFAX HARBOUR 1856

THE ARAB, BRIGANTINE, & THE MILO, BRIG, OFF HALIFAX HARBOUR, 1856

I gave them two for the price of one.
The *Arab* and *Milo* coming home,
flying the flag of Esson, Boak and Co.,
loaded no doubt with West Indian rum.
They clewed up their sails, like the skirts of girls
picking periwinkles along the strand;
two shore boats rowed out to clear customs
(white flashes of light licking their transoms).
The soldiers' peaked tents on George's Island,
the Martello tower standing guard
like a chess piece over the sea road;
the wind easterly, the sun setting,
the last light aloft in the sails.
I painted this scene for me, defying
the formula, "under all plain sail,"
not giving a goddamn if they hung it.

If you can do this, even once, what the hell else matters?
But, O'Brien, if you give them one masterpiece,
they want another and another. They will hound
you all your days—blaming the black rum, the Black Dog,
forgetting that even one miracle
is too many to expect.

Halifax Yacht Club, Regatta, with Receiving Ship, Pyramus, 1857

"THE FINE ARTS—A large and beautiful painting may be
seen at Wetmore's, representing THE PYRAMUS, receiving
ship, and part of the Dartmouth shore, having in the foreground
the twenty-one yachts comprising the Halifax Yacht Club.
This splendid picture, by young John O'Brien, does the artist
infinite credit. It has been painted for the Club Room, and the
design, drawing, colouring and effect of the whole is worthy of
the spirited association to which it belongs. We are right glad
to learn that young O'Brien is about to visit Europe, where he
will receive one year's tuition in Marine painting. Few persons
have a stronger natural talent for this branch of the fine arts than
O'Brien and we expect to see him return to his native land an
accomplished artist."

It was a good passage, the wind following.
For the first time, I saw my true subject—
the sea! Not the ship, the sky, but the sea
coiling in long grey skeins, crossed
by threads of white spume, flecks of seabirds,
waves shuttling back and forth. The sea,
protean fabric of interwoven marines,
remaking itself, infinitely.
It was at sea I was born and reborn.

Ireland tipped up, a greenish haze
        on the horizon,
then the mountains of Wales, at last
        Liverpool,
home of Rotten-row and Booble-alley,
like all great cities, din and bustle.

O'Brien, did you hear the baleful
Bell-Buoy at the mouth of the Mersey
that made Melville muse on the dead
sleeping "at the bottom of the deep?"
Or were your ears and eyes
trained only on the future?
As you wrote your dear father,
coming to Europe would make you
what you wished to be, "viz., an artist."
But O'Brien, you already were,
you were.

J.W. Carmichael on 'The Art Of Marine Painting In Oil Colours'

"Begin with the sky,
weaken the colour
as you approach the horizon.

Paint the clouds
with Cologne earth,
madder lake, and cobalt.

Let light penetrate the foresea.
Touch the thin crests
of the waves

with raw sienna,
the same colour
as the sky.

For the distant land,
cobalt or ultramarine
and purple madder—

for the lights of the houses,
quays, and forts,
madder lake and yellow ochre—

for the trees, a little burnt sienna.

Remove the houses
to a distance,
paint the hulls

of vessels
with lampblack.
Cover the dark sail

with madder lake,
raw sienna,
mummy.

Give them what they see."

11 November 1857

Dear Father:—

My master, J. W. Carmichael, Esq.,
is not long back from the Baltic Campaign.
His work in the *Illustrated London News*
was known to me. All said I could not find
a better teacher. In my first work he found
little to correct—why then had I come?
"The fresh sea, midday, with a blue streak
      in the sky"
is his credo. "Give them what they see,
or want to see," he says, "then they will buy."

You can see there was little to learn
in England—that is, until I saw Turner:
The Shipwreck and *Dutch Boats in a Gale.*
Carmichael's seas are a grand monotony,
while Turner's are "a dizzy whirl of rushing,
writhing, tortured rage," as Ruskin says,
"an anarchy of enormous power."
The sky is roiling soot as if all the chimneys
of London belched their brimstone smoke at once.

The northern seas are crushed beneath this weather,
men, women and boats mere flotsam.
The rescue boat circles the maelstrom;
behind looms the dismasted wreck.
It is impossible to know whether
the world is being drowned or resurrected.
Avalanche, deluge, shipwreck and fire—
as Hazlitt said, "They are pictures of nothing."

Upon first seeing Turner—vertigo!
Did you feel yourself go under, O'Brien,
a drowning man sucking his last innocent breath?

SCOTIA, OFF LIZARD POINT, ENGLAND, 1858

I painted my own departure—land's end—
passing Lizard Point, the barque *Scotia*
close-hauled on the starboard tack, topsails reefed.
My homecoming was a harbinger.
The sea piqued by an unrelenting swell,
rolling from Newfoundland to Ireland.
I said goodbye to calm waters, as England
      fell behind.
I now sailed into storms, contrary winds.
I arrived on the shores of New Scotia,
a bona fide master, but forgotten
already by ships' captains, the good citizens,
the press who once praised me so freely.

Ah, O'Brien, there are always the Irish
by whatever name. Now our masters
have no borders. There is no New World
where we might start over—
but for art, that far country.

PORTRAIT OF THE ARTIST

J. O'BRIEN, ARTIST, NO. 9 JACOB STREET
INSTRUCTIONS GIVEN IN LANDSCAPE
AND MARINE PAINTING.
15 NOVEMBER 1858

So, O'Brien, you set up shop
beside the shoemaker, butcher
and joiner, only to find
men needed shoes to walk in,
meat to eat, chairs to sit in,
but not another seer in this garrison town;
only to find you were one of a kind.

NEW PHOTOGRAPH GALLERY
VICTORIA BLOCK, HOLLIS STREET
W. CHASE,
Mr. C. has the assistance of Mr. John O'Brien in
the colouring of Photographs, some fine specimens
of which may be seen at the Rooms.
April 30, 1859

Now I find you in the Photograph and Ambrotype Gallery,
above the tailor shop on Hollis:
a colourist, bathed in nitrates,
mercury,
mad as a hatter,
tinting the literal.

[*62*]

I opened my eyes like lenses
and a colloidal light flooded in.
I counted: one, two, three, four, five, six,
but no image took form. My room dissolved,
the corners, colours, hard edges blurred—
I was as blind as a photograph.

I've been looking for you, O'Brien,
leafing through the archives, the old albums,
coming up blank.
For two decades you disappeared,
half blind or drunk, or blind drunk,
who knows?
I've been looking for you, O'Brien,
down by the freight sheds at Richmond Station,
next to the Narrows Bridge. (They say you lived there,
"at the railway," with the pigs, goats, cows,
the poultry and the poor running the streets.)
The boxcars balance on the bridge,
the engine enters its house.
Is that you leaning against a telegraph pole,
loitering, watching the lorry traffic,
a bowler on your pate?

They say you were tall,
well built,
but there is no self-portrait.

I looked for you on the stoop
of R.H. Cogswell, Optician:
they say your eyes went bad ("impaired vision?")
after painting the banners for the Catholic Temperance Society—
penance or punishment, O'Brien?
Is that you, a dandy, tall, with moustache and mutton chops,
suited in striped pants and tunic,
that bowler cocked on your head—
myopic, staring down
the camera,
the future?

The photographer
seeks vacancy
in the morning light,
before business,
the streets deserted
as if after a disaster,
seeks stasis,
not the movement
of a ship into the wind,
the sea's chaos.

Don't move, O'Brien,
or you will blur
into oblivion.

I want to see your face,
but I find only your half-brother, James J. O'Brien,
in cameo, a member of the School Board, 1884–1885,
a handsome man, bright-eyed and ginger-bearded
(though perhaps the sepia deceives),
smiling, perhaps a little self-satisfied.
What did he think of you, the older brother,
drunkard, down and out?
Perhaps there was no resemblance.

I've been looking for you in all the wrong places.
I should have been diving into darkness,
where the camera could not go,
into the Blue Bell Tavern.
I might have found you there,
"a flaming nuisance,"
another "unfortunate."

You might have found me there, at the Black Dog
or the Bowling Saloon, quaffing a Keith's.
I cursed the camera, its alchemy.
If the captains wanted a still picture

they could have it. I would paint the ship
in a storm, the shipwreck—their nightmare.
Let the camera capture that, I'd say,
ordering another India Pale Ale.

Where were all my ships? Gone to China,
scuttled there by the steamers from the Clyde.
Foreign artists copped my commissions.
I could no longer afford fine linen,
had to scumble my poor pigment on sailcloth
          (there's an irony!).
See the City Directory: there I am,
Artist and Decorative Painter.
Come to this—curlicues, vignettes, frescoes—
but at least I had a brush in my hands.

I had become that other brother,
my dark double risen from the deep.
He followed me, tavern to tavern,
his skull barnacled, trailing seaweed hair,
salt water sloshing in his boots and lungs,
voice garbled and shrill as a gull's,
I started awake when he whispered our name,
smelled the dankness where he slept inside me.

Who doesn't have a dark brother
who wakes him with whispers of doubt,
who tells him to abandon hope,
who steals away in the middle of the night
to commit mayhem?
In the morning my heart says,
start again,

if it's not too late already.
We keep going on, O'Brien,
what else can we do?
I know, I know.

FISHERMAN IN A
MOUNTAIN LANDSCAPE, 1879

Father dead. "Well known ... respected," the papers said.
I, too, was well known—respected never!
They would rather praise the water-colourist,
the floral cameo, the topographic view.
I painted a roundel in his memory,
a fisherman in a mountain landscape.
There are no mountains here, except in name,
but as a boy he might have known such a place.
I put him where he might have some peace.
He lived long enough to see me fail,
the promising son, washed up at thirty.

We, too, abandoned you,
O'Brien, our native son,
blaming the alcohol,
the darkroom chemicals,
the black Irish mood.
A collective turning away.
We did not wish to see
the ship in peril,
the underbelly
of our enterprise.
Spare us the drama,
give us the clean line,
everything shipshape—
the sea becalmed
as if Christ himself
had walked there.

Record of the Shipping
of Yarmouth, N.S.

"The records of the progress of any locality are generally full of
interest to its inhabitants; but to a community whose principal
source of prosperity has always been found in the extension of
maritime enterprise, these records at once possess a more general
and varied interest,—for the lives of those "who go down to the
sea in ships, that do business in great waters," have always been
connected with thrilling adventure, daring exploit, and noble self-
denial. To the "sails that whiten every sea" is civilization indebted
for that commerce which is the life of the nations; and while
these argosies of trade are ever contributing to the sustenance of
mankind, it is with a feeling of pride that we can point to the
maritime enterprise that has characterized Yarmouth from the
first year of her existence. This compilation shows that today she
stands unrivalled among the Ports of the world in the value of
tonnage of her Shipping proportionate to her population."

Odd to think, you walked
my home streets, in Yarmouth town,
cowled as usual in pea soup fog
so thick it collapses time itself:
jacks-of-all-trades intoxicated by the sea,
we might have emerged through penumbrae
billowing from the harbour,
like shadowy figures in pawnshop daguerreotypes—
anonymous yet somehow familiar—

might have passed through each other,
our bodies offering no resistance,
atoms mixing in the swirling droplets.

You were lost, O'Brien,
rudderless in winter seas.
Perhaps you read in the provincial dailies
or Dominion guidebooks
about those enterprising Yarmouthians—
off to load oil in Philadelphia,
guano from the bird islands of Peru,
hides from the gauchos of La Plata,
sugar and exotic goods from the Far East.

Perhaps, you thought, there would be a commission;
here you could make a new start,
paint some "gay and gallant barque"
for parlour or office,
and stay clear of the gin houses.

But such was your luck, O'Brien,
to arrive in 1879, the year
that thirty-one ships went down,
one hundred and six souls were lost,
the economy was on the skids.

I can see you now, hanging
about the wharves and boardwalks,
trying to look respectable
in your threadbare suit,
in need of a good meal
and a hard drink,
offering to paint a ship portrait, or trace
a grapevine design on a lorry chassis.
Repairing at the end of the day to Fag End
to flop at the Phoenix Hotel,
a.k.a. Vengeance House,
home to jacks-in-port
and whores.

THE WILLIAM LAW, SHIP, 1879

William Law, businessman, shipowner, agent
for the Boston Marine Insurance Company,
to humour me, handed me a zinc plate
with the words *G. H. Porter, Auctioneer*,
already lettered on it, and said, "Here,
since you're such a fine artist, paint me a sign."

And so I did: the *William Law*, Ship.
I crammed that vessel (the largest ever
built in Yarmouth County) into a square frame,
made the best of a bad situation:
my art gibbeted, for all to see,
swinging in the wind on Cliff Street.

What failing did you possess, O'Brien,
besides a wish to please?
As Ruskin said, "A painter of men
must be among men,
but as watcher
not companion."

ARGYLE, BARQUE: DEPARTURE & CAPSIZE, 1880

Lawson solicited an illustration
for his book—that litany of lost vessels
    (six hundred in all)—
one damn disaster after another.
Which calamity to record? I chose
a stereoscopic view of the *Argyle*—
this twin vision being all the rage—
its departure and its capsize on Squam Beach.

— PANEL I —

There she goes, past Forchu, all sails drawing.
Captain and mate bid farewell from the aft deck,
glad no doubt to see the land fall behind.
Chimney smoke trails from the lightkeeper's house,
the last they will see of home and hearth.
A sailor's red warning flags the sky.

"NARRATIVE OF THE WRECK OF THE BARQUE ARGYLE, CAPTAIN JAMES BURTON, AND THE LOSS OF ALL HANDS EXCEPT ONE."

"The shock was sudden—the waves immediately began to break over the vessel with terrific fury, and those on board, eleven in number, were compelled to seek safety in the rigging ... after six terrible hours of agony and suffering, during which they were drenched with spray and exposed to the piercing winter wind, the day began to break ... At twelve o'clock one of the sailors fell from his place on the foretop, and, striking on the deck, was killed. He was afterwards found on the beach, with the front part of his skull broken in ... All the bodies were found before Tuesday night, some of them eleven miles from the scene of the wreck ..."

In my mind's eye, the *Argyle* was a whale.
The sea became a mouth, the furious beak
of the monster kraken, wrapping sucking arms
around her, swallowing the vessel whole.
They said, I found my ships at the bottom
of a bottle, not the sea. "Jonah," they joked,
when the years swallowed me, spat me out.
　　　"Better JOB," I said.

In the end, O'Brien, as you said,
it was not ships but lives you painted—
their rosy departures and dark homecomings.

The Plymouth, Barque, 1881

For a time it seemed fortunes might reverse.
My portraits were again in demand.
I painted the *Maida* and the *Plymouth*
(this last for the great shipbuilders of Hantsport),
her sails half reefed under darkening sky,
keel cutting the corrugated sea on the port tack.
Seeing her, I could almost believe again
      in a golden age.
But all around me ships were sinking,
steam was stealing away the cargoes
      of the Novascotiamen.
As the paint dried I was already bound
      for the Poor House.

And we right along with you, O'Brien,
now that we were turning inland,
our fortunes run out of town on rails
into the dry-footed confederation—
the ships run aground to rot
up muddy creeks.

ENTERING HALIFAX HARBOUR, 1881

I, too, looked inward, inside the harbour
that had always been my anteroom.
The little ferry shuttled shore to shore,
men rowed and sailed their home-built boats
like emissaries of my own affairs.
The city grew around me, unaware
of my foundering prospects, failing vision.
Still, ships entered my life, looming out
          of the fog,
magnificent, in proportion to my misery.

If not for your eyes, O'Brien,
the harbour, circa 1880,
might never have existed.
Without an image, the past is lost,
like a ship "not afterward heard of."

Your paintings are celebrated
in the city's galleries,
the harbour fills with gay sails,
again people throng the wharves
to gawk at your stock in trade.

Too late, dead already a hundred years.

We walk through the hurricane-felled forest,
where Juan flattened the white pines,
as did the unnamed wind
that blew as you lay on your deathbed.
We look seaward as the tall ships
cruise past Point Pleasant, dip once more
below the horizon out by Sambro.
We wish to sail away, it seems,
from our shore-bound lives,
like those who went before,

who walked from Bluenose deck
to Bluenose deck,
down in Montevideo or New York.
We look to the blue horizon
for a new beginning,
some old truth about ourselves.

Too late, dead already a hundred years.

We look to you, O'Brien.

TRIPTYCH: A BARQUE AT SUNRISE;
A BARQUE IN A STORM;
DERELICT BARQUE AT SUNRISE, 1887

The barque is unnamed, anonymous as me.
Dark waters gather under her keel,
drawing her down into the lightless abyss.
Gone are my lyrical violets and blues.
Like my old master, Turner, I scumble
together the greys and greens—the true colours
       of sky and water.

Some say I blinded myself with bad booze,
but did they consider I saw too much,
       not too little?

In triptychs I told my common story:
departure—stormy passage—abandon.
I drifted into old age, my will broken,
reputation in tatters—a wreck
menacing the melancholic Atlantic.
In the end, after the graveyard watch,
the sky cracked open like old canvas,
a blinding light exploded from the gloom,
the light I first saw in London, in Turner,
when I still believed in the future.

So in the end, we must
become our subject, O'Brien,
as you said.
You were a ship,
rocked in the sea's cradle,
marked for disaster.
Art demands I become you—
your double, that lost brother—
charting the sad particulars
of early promise, long decline.
In the end, you became all of us,
watching the ships sail away,
not, as we thought, into the future
but forever into the past.
We disparage you, O'Brien,
because your failure
is our own,
the whole culture
turned in
upon itself,
peninsular,
forsaking the wide oceans
where our fortunes
were made and lost.

HMS GALATEA, STEAMSHIP, IN A CYCLONE
1888

7 September 1891

MONDAY NIGHT'S STORM
A Large Part of the Narrow's Bridge Carried Away—The Grain Elevator Damaged—A Vessel Sinks in the Harbor—Several Yachts and Schooners Badly Broken Up

The acid had boiled up from my gut
(too much tobacco, booze and bad luck)
corroding my throat until I choked.
I took refuge at my widowed sister's,
lay dying above the Central Engine House,
across the street from the Town Clock,
ticking my life away in its black arms.

At nine o'clock, hurricane winds unwound
from the southeast, unleashing torrents.
Time itself turned counterclockwise,
recoiled into Halifax harbour like the cyclone
that laid the *Galatea* on beam ends,
just as I painted her in the China Sea

—descending into the storm's roiled, green gut,
the gibbous moon witness to disaster
behind a scrim of doom-driven cloud
the colour of entrails; albatross,
those unlucky birds, riding the rogue waves.

The city foundered:
pedestrians crawled up Citadel Hill,
fire alarm bells rang,
the grain elevator chute crashed
            to the docks.
At midnight, the Narrows Bridge
began to sway, a drunken span,
—like you, O'Brien, lurching home—
until trestle and track collapsed.

Across old Scotia
dykes were breached,
orchards uprooted,
the apple crop on the ground;
trees and fences blown down;
two men drowned;
schooners dragged their anchors—

Neptune's revenge
for scorning a sea⁄born son.

Two hours later, the wind was gone
and with it you, O'Brien,
listed in the obits as "Barber."

Life is shipwreck in the end.

> But as old Ruskin mused,
> society destroys the artist,
> always—never the art.

And what is spoken of me?

> When I see a ship, O'Brien,
> it is your portrait I see.

ACKNOWLEDGEMENTS

The author gratefully acknowledges the support of the Nova Scotia Department of Tourism, Culture and Heritage, Culture Division, for a Creation Grant which allowed him the time to work on this poem. ❡ I am deeply grateful for the sharp eye, ear, wit and pencil of my editor, Amanda Jernigan. ❡ The book would not have been possible without the scholarship of Patrick Condon Laurette's *John O'Brien, 1831–91*, published by the Art Gallery of Nova Scotia, 1984. It was this exhibition catalogue that first alerted me to John O'Brien's art and to the importance of his life in the larger story of Nova Scotia's Age of Sail. Furthermore, Laurette's insights were critical to the framing of the poem's narrative. The comprehensive bibliography he compiled led me to many primary sources, especially in the Public Archives of Nova Scotia. I am also grateful to Eric Ruff, Curator of the Yarmouth County Museum, for sharing his expertise on ship portraiture and for showing me the O'Brien portraits in the museum's collection. Similarly, I am grateful to Mora Dianne O'Neill, curator of historical prints and drawings, Art Gallery of Nova Scotia, who shared with me the O'Brien portraits in the gallery's permanent collection, especially *The Arab, Brigantine, and The Milo, Brig, Off Halifax Harbour, 1856*. ❡ The quotations from "The Abstract of the log of the Barque *Stag*" were compiled by Harry Piers and are held in the Public Archives of Nova Scotia, as are many other primary documents relating to the ships O'Brien painted. ❡ Principal sources on the lives of Irish Catholics in 19th-century Ireland, on the laws governing them, and on the Potato Famine and the Irish emigration to Canada, were *The Irish in Nova Scotia, Annals of the Charitable Irish Society of Halifax (1786–1836)*, by Herbert Leslie Stewart (Kentville, Nova Scotia: Kentville Publishing Co. Ltd., 1950), and *Flight From Famine, The Coming of the Irish to Canada*, by Donald McKay (Toronto: McClelland & Stewart, 1990). The term "Irish Janus" is attributed to author and genealogist Terence Punch. The words of John Uniacke, Attorney General of Nova

Scotia ("The Irish emigrant ..."), are quoted by McKay, who cites the Reports of the Select Committee, House of Lords, on the Colonization from Ireland. Uniacke was arguing against improving conditions aboard emigrant ships. The quotation beginning, "Unless the Irish go away ..." is also taken from McKay and attributed to an anonymous speaker. ⟨ A number of passages are taken from works by Herman Melville: "Dirge-like swell" is from *Typee*; "at the bottom of the deep" is from *Redburn*. "I prefer not to" is the refrain of "Bartleby The Scrivener" from the short story of the same name. ⟨ In "29 November 1852," *kaloolah* is Polynesian for "rover." ⟨ Quotes by John Ruskin are taken from *Modern Painters*, except "a painter of men ..." which is from *The Stones of Venice*. ⟨ Passages from "Narrative of the Wreck of the Barque *Argyle*" are taken from *Record of the Shipping of Yarmouth, N.S.* by J. Murray Lawson, 1876. ⟨ Objects (ivory backscratcher, Shanghai, etc.) referred to in the section "We still have our Water Streets ..." were donated to the Yarmouth County Museum by Kathryn Ladd. They were acquired by her parents, Fred and Grace (Forrest) Ladd, on their voyages aboard the steel-hulled barque *Belmont*, the last of Yarmouth's commercial tall ships. ⟨ As well, various newspapers of the day are quoted. ⟨ The reproductions on page 2 are of John O'Brien's *MICMAC, Ship, 1853* (Collection of the Art Gallery of Nova Scotia; gift of the Estate of Arthur D. Stairs, Halifax, Nova Scotia, 1993) ⟨ The reproduction on page 23 is of John O'Brien's *Halifax Harbour, Sunset, c. 1853* (Collection the Metropolitan Halifax Chamber of Commerce, Halifax, Nova Scotia, 1989; on loan to the Art Gallery of Nova Scotia). ⟨ The reproduction on page 49 is of John O'Brien's *The ARAB, Brigantine, and the MILO, Brig, off Halifax Harbour, 1856* (Collection of the Art Gallery of Nova Scotia, gift of Judith A. and Alex W. Doyle, Sidney, British Columbia, 1999). ⟨ The reproduction on page 87 is of John O'Brien's *HMS GALATEA, Steamship, in a Cyclone, 1888* (Collection of the Art Gallery of Nova Scotia).

Gaspereau Press acknowledges the support of the
Canada Council for the Arts, the Nova Scotia Department of
Tourism, Culture & Heritage and the Government of Canada
through the Book Publishing Industry Development Program.

Typeset in Poliphilus & Blado by Andrew Steeves
and printed offset at Gaspereau Press.

1   3   5   7   6   4   2

Library and Archives Canada Cataloguing in Publication

Thurston, Harry, 1950–
A ship portrait / Harry Thurston.
Poems.
ISBN 1-55447-007-2 (BOUND)
ISBN 1-55447-006-4 (PBK)
1. O'Brien, John, 1831–1891—Poetry. 2. Harbors—Nova
Scotia—Poetry. I. Title.
PS8589.H88S55 2005   C811'.54   C2005-903495-5

GASPEREAU PRESS PRINTERS & PUBLISHERS
47 CHURCH AVENUE, KENTVILLE, NOVA SCOTIA
CANADA B4N 2M7   WWW.GASPEREAU.COM